THE DINO WHO SAVED CHRISTMAS

WRITTEN BY
MANDA MAC

ILLUSTRATED BY
KEV PAYNE

TO MY INCREDIBLE FAMILY AND FRIENDS, YOUR SUPPORT MEANS EVERYTHING.

I OWE A SPECIAL THANKS TO GLENYS NELLIST FOR HER INVALUABLE EDITING AND INSIGHT.

Hardback ISBN: 978-1-961383-03-6
Library of Congress Control Number: 2023916951

Copyright © 2023 by Manda Mac for Risen Faith Writing LLC
Illustrations by Kev Payne

Risen Faith Writing, L.L.C.
P.O. Box 214
Hernando, MS 38632

All rights reserved.

No part of this publication may be reproduced, distributed, or transmitted in any form or by any means, including photocopying, recording, or other electronic or mechanical methods, without the prior written permission of the publisher, except as permitted by U.S. copyright law. For permission requests, contact Risen Faith Writing LLC
Scripture quotations are taken from the Holy Bible, New Living Translation, copyright ©1996, 2004, 2015 by Tyndale House Foundation. Used by permission of Tyndale House Publishers, Carol Stream, Illinois 60188. All rights reserved.

"Breaking News! Christmas is canceled. It's the week before Christmas, and Santa Claws has announced his retirement due to losing his Christmas spirit."

Bronto Brody spat out his orange juice. "Noooo! Santa Claws can't retire. Who will bring us toys?"

"We just need to help Santa Claws get his spirit back. It's a long way to the North Pole, and there's a blizzard. Let's go!" said Deino Dylan.

"Saber!" Bronto Brody called out to their pet sabertooth tiger.

They raced through the snowy woods and hills.

They dashed around the bend.

Presents went flying!
Saber had crashed into Mrs. Mammoth's cart.

"Oh no! We didn't mean to run into you, Mrs. Mammoth."

They all scrambled to pick up the gifts.

"It's important to slow down during Christmas, or we may forget the true meaning," Mrs. Mammoth said.

"Gifts aren't the true meaning. Jesus is," Deino Dylan chimed in.

Mrs. Mammoth nodded. "That's right. Remember that Jesus is the real reason for Christmas."

"He is the greatest gift of all."

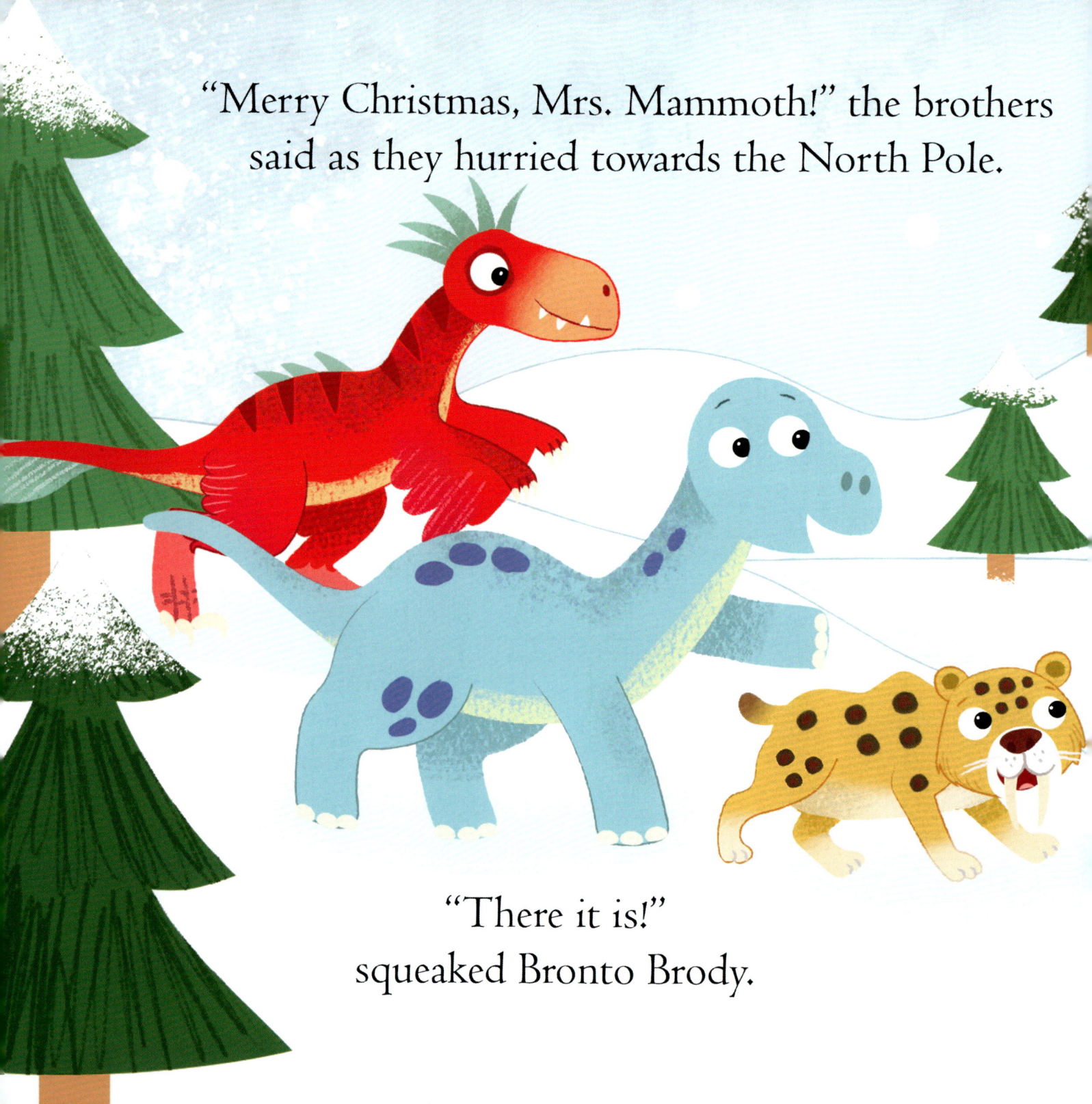

"Merry Christmas, Mrs. Mammoth!" the brothers said as they hurried towards the North Pole.

"There it is!" squeaked Bronto Brody.

"The North Pole!" Deino Dylan said in awe.
KNOCK! KNOCK! KNOCK!

The door opened, and there stood Santa Claws. "Santa Claws! We came to help you find your Christmas spirit." Bronto Brody shivered.

"Y'all must be cold out in this blizzard. Come on in. Let's get y'all warmed up."

They stood by the cozy fire.

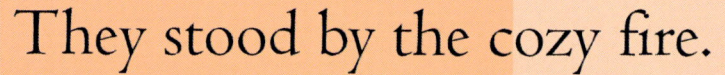

"There's not much time," said Bronto Brody. "We must hurry if we're going to find Santa Claws' Christmas spirit!"

They looked HIGH!

They looked LOW!

They searched every nook and corner.

They couldn't find Santa Claws' Christmas spirit anywhere.
What if his Christmas spirit was lost forever?

Aha! Deino Dylan thought.

"I've got it! We can't find your Christmas spirit, because it's invisible."

"Huh?" Bronto Brody and Santa Claws said together.

"The Christmas spirit lives INSIDE us.
We can't see it.
We must find out why Santa Claws lost it."

"What happened when you
lost the Christmas spirit?"

"I dropped my Christmas cookies."

"Then what?"

"I spilled my milk."

"Did you get new cookies and milk?"

"No, because I felt like my Christmas spirit disappeared."
Bronto Brody knew what to do!

"All we need to do is get Santa new milk and cookies!"

Santa Claws sighed. "I guess it can't hurt to try."

They headed to the kitchen. "There's not much time. We must hurry."

Bronto Brody mixed.

Santa Claws baked.

And Deino Dylan decorated.

Deino Dylan grabbed Santa Claws a glass of milk. The moment of truth came.

Santa ate a cookie, then drank his milk.
They waited.
Santa sighed. Nothing happened.

Bronto Brody thought for a minute. Dropped cookies and spilled milk didn't make Santa Claws lose his Christmas spirit.

How would Santa Claws find the spirit if they couldn't see what made it disappear?

As Bronto Brody looked at the bag of gifts in the corner, he remembered what Mrs. Mammoth had said.

"That's it! Santa, why do you give gifts to the kids on Christmas Day?"

"Because they love them," Santa Claws replied.

"But I thought we gave gifts at Christmastime to remember Jesus, the greatest gift of all," Bronto Brody said.

"That's right! Thanks for reminding me that Jesus is the true meaning of Christmas," Santa Claws exclaimed. And suddenly, he was overcome with joy and the spirit of Christmas.

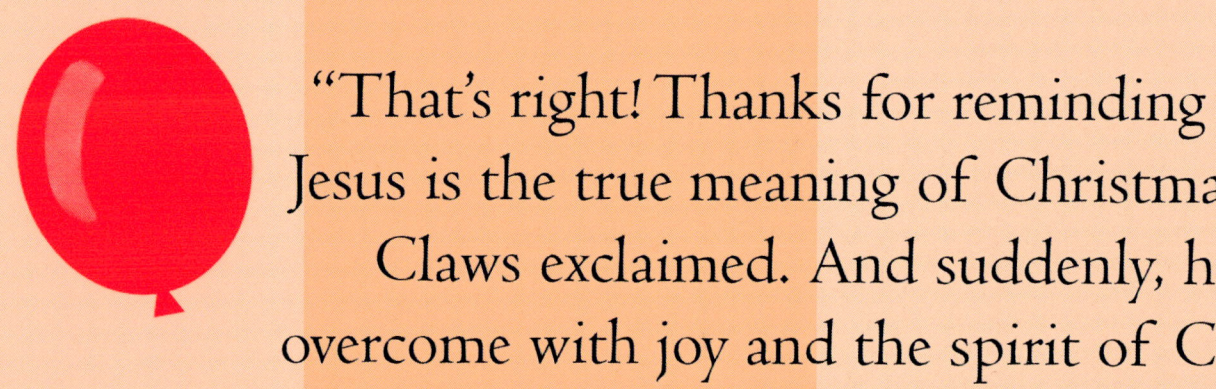

Santa Claws' gifts remind us that Jesus came to save us, and that's the greatest gift of all.

Santa Claws called out cheerfully,
"Merry Christmas to all, and to all a goodnight!"

ABOUT THE AUTHOR

Manda Mac lives in North Mississippi with her husband,
two sons, 4 dogs, cat, bearded dragon, and horse.
She is a preschool homeschool teacher to her 4-year-old.
Her passion is to follow God's plan (Jeremiah 29:11)
and to use her gift to write about God
in unique ways that will interest young readers.